Effective
Team Building

David Goose

Effective Team Building
by David Goose

ISBN 978-1-926917-09-2

Printed in the United States of America

Copyright © 2010 Psylon Press

All rights reserved. Except for use in a review, no portion of this book may be reproduced in any form without the express written permission of the author. For information regarding permission, write to admin@psylonpress.com

Neither the author nor the publisher assumes any responsibility for the use or misuse of information contained in this book.

Other books by Psylon Press:

100% Blonde Jokes
R. Cristi
ISBN 978-0-9866004-1-8

Choosing a Dog Breed Guide
Eric Nolah
ISBN 978-0-9866004-5-6

Best Pictures Of Paris
Christian Radulescu
ISBN 978-0-9866004-8-7

Best Gift Ideas For Women
Taylor Timms
ISBN 978-0-9866004-4-9

Top Bikini Pictures
Taylor Timms
ISBN 978-0-9866426-3-0

Cross Tattoos
Johnny Karp
ISBN 978-0-9866426-4-7

Beautiful Breasts Pictures
Taylor Timms
ISBN 978-1-926917-01-6

For more books please visit:
www.psylonpress.com

Contents

Introduction   7

Principles of Team Building   9
Why is Team Building Important?   10
Do you Need Team Building?   11
Steps for Building an Effective Team   12

Understanding Team Dynamics   13
Recognizing Team Dynamics   15
Constructively Managing Team Dynamics   15
Steps for Effective Team Problem Solving   17
Team Player Styles   18
Contributors   18
Collaborators   18
Communicators   19
Challengers   19
Identifying Team Player Styles   20
Maximizing Team Meeting Effectiveness   24
Is a Meeting Really Necessary?   24
Meeting Facilitating   25
Attending Meetings   25

Team Building for Leaders and Managers   27
Leading Instead of Bossing   29
Team Communication   30
Team Motivation   32

Elements of Productive Teams   35
Resource Allocation   36

Cooperation	36
Communication	37

Team Building Exercises 39

Team Building Exercises	41
Back to Back Drawing	42
Survival	43
Eliminating Labeling	43
The Human Spring	44
The Mine Field	44
Massage Circle	45
The Human Knot	45
Stranded on an Island	46
Roses and Thorns	46
Hula Hoop	46
The Bridge	47
Pat on the Back	47

Ice Breakers for Team Building 49

Two Truths and a Lie	50
Toilet Paper Game	50
Interview and Introductions	51
Animals	51
The Last Line	51
Line Up	52
Name Game	52
Orange Pass	52
Styrofoam Tower	53
Scavenger Hunt	53
Questions	54

Team Building Ideas and Activities 57

Team Progress Boards	58

Team Incentives/Bonuses	58
Team News	58
Team Name	58
T-shirts	59
Group Activities	59
Group Lunch	59
Retreats	59
Social Outings	59
Sports	60

Mistakes to Avoid — **61**

Team Effectiveness Critique	63
Team Building Needs Assessment	65
Team Focus Assessment	67
Work Satisfaction Inventory	69

Introduction

Team building is a continual process that assists a work group in evolving into a cohesive team unit. The members of the team share not only expectations for accomplishing tasks as a group but also learn to support and trust one another and respect individual differences in one another.

A team can take on a decided life of its own and the goal of a team builder is to maintain and nurture that team on a regular basis, much in the same way that individual employees would be nurtured and supported.

Good team building skills makes it possible to unite employees around a common, central goal and also to generate improved productivity.

Let's get started!

Chapter 1

Principles of Team Building

Why is Team Building Important ?

Team building can sometimes be given a low priority because they do not consider the many advantages and benefits that can come about from a team effort that is well executed.

The benefits of team building can include:
• Goals that are realistic and achievable for both the team and the individual members of the team.
• Leaders and employees are able to commit to supporting one another for the team.
• Team members are able to understand priorities and support when another when needed.
• Communication remains open, allowing for the expression of new ideas, articulation of problems and improved work methods.
• More effective problem solving.
• Increased meaning to performance feedback as team members learn what is expected and are able to monitor their own performance against those expectations.
• Conflict is understood as an opportunity to resolve problems through open discussion.
• Members are encouraged to try out new ideas.
• Team members learn to work more effectively as a team unit.
• Good communication between team members and individuals.
• Increased creativity and productivity.
• Motivation of team members to achieve goals.
• A climate of collaborative problem solving and cooperation.

- Increased levels of commitment and job satisfaction.
- Improved levels of support and trust.
- Diverse co-workers working well together.
- Establishment of clear work objectives.
- Improved operating procedures and policies.

Do you Need Team Building ?

How do you know if your team is in need of team building? One thing to keep in mind is that most teams can always benefit from team building, but the following symptoms could signal that your team has a more immediate need for team building:

- Decreased productivity
- Hostility or conflicts among staff members
- Confusion about relationships, assignments, etc.
- Lack of involvement or apathy
- Decisions not carried through properly or understood
- Complaints of favoritism or discrimination
- Lack of imagination, initiation, innovation
- Low participation, ineffective staff meetings
- Negative reactions to management

Steps for Building an Effective Team

The most important rule of team building is to establish leadership within each team member. The most effective and successful teams are built upon relationships based on loyalty and trust instead of fear. Keep the following steps in mind as you approach team building:

- Each member's ideas are valuable.
- Communication must be clear with directives clarified.
- Cooperation and trust must be encouraged.
- Team members must be encouraged to share information with the contribution of all members emphasized.
- Problem solving tasks should be delegated to the team.
- Communication should be facilitated by remaining open to concerns and suggestions, asking questions and offering help.
- Team goals and values must be established; with team performance evaluated through the discussion of progress toward goals.
- The team should have a clear idea of what needs to be accomplished.
- Consensus should be used for setting objectives, solving problems and planning for action.
- Ground rules for the team should be established to ensure success and efficiency.
- Brainstorming and listening should be encouraged.

Chapter 2

Understanding Team Dynamics

Team dynamics are those forces which operate within a team or between different groups of people.

These dynamics are often unseen but can strongly influence the way in which the team behaves, performs and reacts. As a result, team dynamics can be extremely complex.

Consider the following example. There is a small team of six individuals working in one office. Within this group there are two people who have a strong friendship. This friendship would be considered to be a natural force and that force could have an influence on the remainder of the team; which could be either negative or positive.

There are also other factors that can influence a team as well. For instance, sometimes structural elements within the office itself which can create a force that can influence the flow of communication.

In some cases it can even separate a team into sub-groups. It is also possible for a force to be lacking and have an effect on a team dynamic. For instance, if the leader of an office is permanently removed, this could cause the team to respond in a particular manner.

Recognizing Team Dynamics

Team dynamics can be recognized by looking out for the various forces which can influence team behavior. These forces can include:
- Personality styles
- Team roles
- Office layout
- Tools and technology (bulletin board, email, etc.)
- Organizational culture
- Procedures, processes and methodologies

Constructively Managing Team Dynamics

Team dynamics must be managed in the most constructive manner possible. In order to do this it is important to look for the natural forces that may be in play within the team, determine whether those forces are acting positively or negatively and make necessary intervention in order to affect those dynamics in a more positive manner.

For instance, if a wall of cabinets in the office is inhibiting the follow of communication within a team, it would be necessary to re-position that wall and possibly even the layout of the office in order to facilitate communication within the group.

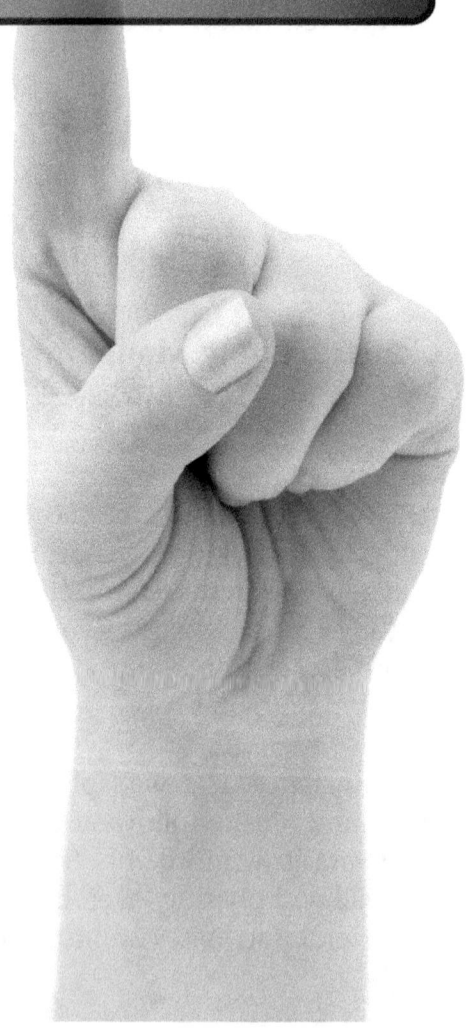

Steps for Effective Team Problem Solving

Begin by defining the objective or the goal. The team should know what should be focused upon.

1. This can be accomplished by laying out the basic objective or goal and then allowing the team to define and expand that objective.

2. The team must also define why the problem must be solved in addition to what must be solved. The team must identify why it is necessary them as well as the organization to achieve this goal. This can be accomplished by asking 'what is the benefit of resolving this problem?'

3. The obstacles that could prevent the team from achieving the objective should also be defined. Focus on internal obstacles rather than external obstacles.

4. The team must also plan specific actions by laying our four to five definite steps that can be taken. These should be written down and should be actions that are observable and measurable.

5. The team must work on changing the obstacles previously identified.

6. Now it is time to take action!

Team Player Styles

In any team there can be a wide variety of different types of team members such as challengers, contributors, communicators, collaborators, etc. Each person is likely to have all four types of team players present within them, but one or two types will usually be more dominate than other types. A successful team should display all four types of team player styles in order to be well rounded.

Contributors

Individuals who are contributors tend to be task oriented people who enjoy providing the team with data and technical information. These individuals will push the team to set higher standards. They tend to be dependable although that can sometimes turn into becoming too weighed down by details; sometimes to the point of missing the big picture. Contributors are usually authoritative, responsible, proficient, reliable and organized.

Collaborators

These individuals are usually very goal oriented who can easily see a mission, goal or objective. They tend to be flexible and will remain open to new ideas. They are also often willing to pitch in and will work outside their defined role without complaint. In addition, they usually have no problem sharing the limelight with others. These individuals are 'big picture' people. They tend to be goal directed, forward looking, flexible, imaginative and accommodating.

Communicators

These individuals are often process oriented. They tend to be effective listeners and are skilled at conflict resolution, involvement, feedback and consensus building. These are people persons who often will not confront others. They tend to be relaxed, considerate, supportive, tactful and enthusiastic.

Challengers

These individuals are often adventurers who will question methods, goals and the ethics of the game. They may disagree with higher authorities and the leader. They are also often risk takers. In some cases they may not recognize when they should back off and could try to push the team too far. They tend to be ethical, principled, outspoken and honest.

Identifying Team Player Styles

The below survey will assist in identifying each individual's style as a team player.

Each item should be answered as honestly as possible regarding how you feel you function as a team member. Items are ranked with 4= most like you, 3=next most like you, 2=next, 1=least like you. All items must be answered.

During team meetings, I typically:
Offer technical information or data	4 3 2 1
Ask questions about methods or goals	4 3 2 1
Ensure everyone is involved	4 3 2 1
Keep everyone focused on the goals or objectives	4 3 2 1

In regards to the team leader, I usually:
Offer advice related to my expertise	4 3 2 1
Suggest that our work should be goal related	4 3 2 1
Try to help build a positive environment	4 3 2 1
Will disagree when I feel it is necessary	4 3 2 1

When I feel stressed, I:
Complain to others	4 3 2 1
Can be too direct in my communication	4 3 2 1
Use humor to reduce tension	4 3 2 1
Lose patience easily	4 3 2 1

When there are conflicts, I typically:
Provide reasons why one side is right	4 3 2 1
See differences as a basis for change	4 3 2 1
Press others for an honest discussion	4 3 2 1
Try to reduce tension with humor	4 3 2 1

Other members of the team see me as:
Flexible	4 3 2 1
Factual	4 3 2 1
Candid	4 3 2 1
Encouraging	4 3 2 1

At times, I can be:
Too laid back	4 3 2 1
Too results oriented	4 3 2 1
Shortsighted	4 3 2 1
Self-righteous	4 3 2 1

When there are problems with the team, I:
Press for a candid discussion	4 3 2 1
Push for increased listening and feedback	4 3 2 1
Work hard to provide better info	4 3 2 1
Suggest we review our mission	4 3 2 1

To me, a risky team contribution is:
Working outside my defined role	4 3 2 1
Questioning the team's work	4 3 2 1
Pushing the team to set higher standards	4 3 2 1
Providing team members with feedback	4 3 2 1

At times, other team members see me as:
A nitpicker   4 3 2 1
A perfectionist   4 3 2 1
Unwilling to assess goals   4 3 2 1
Not serious about getting the
job done   4 3 2 1

I believe that team problem solving should include:
Solid data and info   4 3 2 1
High level listening skills   4 3 2 1
Cooperation by everyone   4 3 2 1
Willingness to ask difficult questions   4 3 2 1

When a new team is formed, I:
Seek to clarify the basic mission   4 3 2 1
Ask questions about goals   4 3 2 1
Try to meet the other members   4 3 2 1
Want to know what is expected of me   4 3 2 1

At times, I may make others feel:
Like they do not care about other
people   4 3 2 1
As though they don't live up to
my standards   4 3 2 1
That they are not as confrontational
as me   4 3 2 1
That they do not think long range   4 3 2 1

I believe the role of the team leader is:
To bring out diverse ideas   4 3 2 1
Create an environment of
participation   4 3 2 1
Help the team establish goals   4 3 2 1

Ensure efficient problem resolution   4 3 2 1

I believe team decisions should be based on:
The weight of the evidence   4 3 2 1
An open assessment   4 3 2 1
A team member consensus   4 3 2 1
The team's goals and mission   4 3 2 1

Sometimes I tend to:
Overemphasize strategic issues   4 3 2 1
Do not see the importance of the team process   4 3 2 1
Play the devil's advocate   4 3 2 1
See the climate of the team as the solution   4 3 2 1

People sometimes describe me as:
Dependable   4 3 2 1
Independent   4 3 2 1
Participative   4 3 2 1
Imaginative   4 3 2 1

Much of the time, I am:
Honest   4 3 2 1
Enthusiastic   4 3 2 1
Committed and flexible   4 3 2 1
Hardworking and responsible   4 3 2 1

When relating to other team members, I Get annoyed because:
They do not work well together   4 3 2 1
They do not review team goals   4 3 2 1
They do not finish on time   4 3 2 1
They object to team actions   4 3 2 1

Maximizing Team Meeting Effectiveness

Meetings can often seem to be a waste of time to many people. As a result they can be unproductive as well as frustrating, especially if they are not executed in the proper manner. Through proper planning, it is possible to reduce the number of meetings as well as the length of meetings while at the same time increasing productivity.

Is a Meeting Really Necessary ?

Prior to holding a meeting, it is important to determine whether you need to even have a meeting or whether the meeting is only being held because of routine. Meetings should always have a specific purpose. Daily meetings are fine as long as they are planned with a specific purpose in mind. If the primary purpose of the meeting is to issue announcements, it would be more efficient to simply send out an email. In addition, it is important to note that team members should only attend meetings if they truly need to be there and the subject of the meeting is relevant to them.

Meeting Facilitating

It is imperative that the meeting facilitator make the most of the meeting by determining what should be accomplished during the meeting ahead of time. Try to stick to the goals of the meeting and void including any unrelated goals or objectives. Visual aids and handouts can help in clarifying objectives and keeping the audience's attention. Remember that it is fine to conclude a meeting early but the meeting should never go beyond the scheduled conclusion time.

Attending Meetings

To make the most of a meeting it is important to plan to arrive on time and even a few minutes early when possible. Always bring paper and a pen for jotting down notes. Be an active listener and participant in the meeting by asking appropriate questions. If there is not time during the actual meeting to pose questions, make a point to follow-up with the meeting facilitator after the meeting to pose questions or offer comments.

BOSS

Chapter 3

Team Building for Leaders and Managers

While the participation of all members of a team is critical to building the team, the role of the team leader or manager is also important. The following guidelines can make it easier for the leader/manager to facilitate the building of a team:

- Remember to lead rather than boss others around
- Remain flexible. Be open to new ideas and suggestions
- Give credit to your team and avoid trying to grab all of the glory
- Make a point to award team achievements
- Be sure to involve everyone in the team and do not leave anyone out
- Praise your team in public and make corrections in private

Leading Instead of Bossing

It is important to keep in mind that there is only a fine line between leading your team and bossing them. While it is easier to boss than to lead, leading is more productive. When you boss someone you are simply telling them what to do, whereas leading is much more involved. When you lead your team instead of bossing them, the team will naturally be more productive.

Bossing relies upon authority in order to instill fear into subordinates. This type of behavior can hurt the morale of the team as well as lead to resentment. This is particularly true when the leader or manager does not have confidence in the ability of his team members and feels as though he/she needs to micromanage everything. When a manager feels as though they must micromanage every little thing he or she will naturally spend much of their time supervising the team and will have little time to actually add anything to the team.

A good manager or team leader will have the respect of their team and will be able to inspire confidence within the team. He or she will also trust the members of the team and feel comfortable delegating tasks to team members and give them the freedom to accomplish those tasks in their own way. Because tasks are delegated, the leader/manager will then have more time to contribute to the project/team and will be more productive than if they spend all of their time bossing rather than leading. A good leader will also listen to their team and have an open door policy regarding communication.

Team Communication

A team that is not able to communicate is not really a team it is simply a group of people who are working toward individual goals rather than a central goal. One of the most important keys to a successful team is communication. Without communication it is impossible to exchange instructions,data, information and ideas. A team must have proper communication to function in an effective manner.

It is important to understand that there are actually two sides to communication. One side is the speaker and the other is the listener.

Barriers can arise in communication as a result of the fault of either the speaker or the listener.

The speaker is responsible for conveying his/her message in a manner that is clear and so that the listener can understand. This means the speaker must understand the listener's background and use language that is appropriate for presenting their message. In addition, the listener must make sure they pay careful attention to the details of what is being said.

This means that their full attention must be provided to the speaker. They must avoid trying to do other things while the speaker is talking. Taking notes may help. If the listener does not understand something, questions should be asked for clarification.

Communication should occur within a timely manner. Urgent problems that require immediate attention should be reported to appropriate team members without delay. Team members should be contacted either by person or in phone for extremely urgent matters. When responding to questions, it is better to respond within the shortest amount of time possible. This is particularly true if a team member is reliant upon the answer in order to continue with a task.

A proper balance of communication is essential. Both too much as well as too little communication can cause problems within a team. Too much information can be counter-productive. Not every single detail must be relayed. At the same time, not relaying enough information can also be counterproductive.

It can be helpful to everyone to provide periodic updates on the status of projects.

Team Motivation

It can be a huge task to motivate a team. In the best situation, a team will be naturally energetic and in this case they can be very easy to motivate. Of course, there can also be teams that are somewhat sluggish and in this case it is going to be more difficult to motivate that team. In most instances, a team will be a blend of both because everyone is different and a team is comprised of individuals.

One of the best ways to motivate a team is for the team leader to be motivated. When the team sees the motivation of the team leader, it will naturally rub off on them to varying degrees and inspire them to be motivated. There are also other actors that can affect team motivation. One thing to keep in mind is that most people tend to be more motivated when they feel more comfortable within their work environment. When people are friendly with one another, they work better together and they create personal relationships with one another that create a more positive environment.

Ways in which a team can strengthen their relationships include participating in recreational activities, holding team lunches, team building exercises, etc. An excellent way to motivate a team is to establish goals and create challenges for the team. When people are working toward a common goal it gives them something to focus upon and strive towards. Two different sets of goals can be established; one for the team and one for each member of the team.

Making sure you are appreciative of the work the team does is another way to motivate them. Even something as simple as saying 'please' and 'thank you' can accomplish quite a lot. When a team recognizes that their work and contributions are appreciated, it can serve as a big motivation and they will work harder. Incentives and awards can be given for performance as well as once goals have been met; either by the individuals or the team as a whole.

It should be kept in mind that everyone is different and different methods for motivation can affect different people in different ways. What motivates one person may do nothing for another. This is why it is important for you to spend some time finding out what motivates individual members of your team.

Chapter 4

Elements of Productive Teams

A team that is productive is built upon three critical elements:

- Resource allocation
- Communication
- Cooperation

Resource Allocation

One of the essentials of building a productive team is efficiently allocating resources. The most important resource within a team is the actual team members. Team members must be positioned where the most can be made of their strengths. This will allow the team to be at its strongest. Of course, team members should always work on improving their weaknesses but the team will always be able to work at their greatest potential when the individual member's strengths are maximized.

Cooperation

When cooperation is not present within a team, the productivity of that team can be crippled. Whenever groups of individuals are working only for their own interests or are competing with one another, the functionality of that team can be hindered. While competition in a team impedes the desire to help one another, cooperation makes it possible to form synergies within the team and produce a more constructive and productive environment.

Communication

Communication is essential for team cooperation and efficient resource. The goals of the team must be clearly communicated so that each member of the team understands their tasks. Any problems within the team should be handled through clear communication as well.

Chapter 5

Team Building Exercises

Many teams have been involved in team building activities at some point, whether it was a weekend retreat or an afternoon spent on the golf course or at a rock climbing wall. What happened during the team building exercise should not be the focus but instead what happened when the members of the team returned back to the office. For example, did the team members return to their usual behavior or were they able to better cooperate with one another?

Far too often such activities are planned without any actual thought going into the goals that should be accomplished as a result. Consequently, the entire activity ends up being a waste of time for everyone involved.

Team building exercises can prove to be extremely powerful in terms of uniting a group by developing strengths and addressing weaknesses. This is only possible; however, if the exercises are planned and carried out in a strategic manner. This means there must be true purpose behind the exercise, such as improving the problem solving skills of the team.

The most important element in planning a team building exercise is to determine what it is that is challenging the team. It is only by doing so that you will be able to select the appropriate exercises that will actually benefit the team. Spend some time thinking about the strengths of the team as well as the weaknesses. Consider the following the questions to identify any potential problems:

- Are there any conflicts between particular people that may be creating divisions within the team?
- Do any team members need to get to know one another better?
- Do some members of the team tend to focus on their own successes and cause harm to the group as a result?
- Is poor communication slowing down the progress of the team?
- Do people in the team need to learn how to better work together rather than individually?
- Are some members of the team resistant to change?
- Do some members of the team need a morale boost?

Team Building Exercises

There are hundreds of different team building exercises that can be used for addressing different issues within a team. In this guide a variety of team building exercises will be presented. In determining which team building exercises will be most beneficial consider the following:

- Will the activity achieve the desired change?
- Will all team members participate?
- Will you be able to locate the budget, time and appropriate venue?

- Is there any physical risk involved? If so, you should have a qualified instructor and provide insurance.
- Remember that there should be no psychological risk. All members should be treated with respect and in an equal manner. There should be no humiliation involved. No one should feel excluded.
- Will the activity build openness and trust?
- Are contingency plans in place in case something goes wrong?

Back to Back Drawing

Divide the team into pairs and have each pair sit back to back. Give one person a picture of a shape and the other a pencil and paper pad. Ask the person holding the picture to give their partner verbal instructions on how to draw the shape without actually telling them what it is. Once they have finished, ask the pair to compare their original shape to the actual drawing. After analyzing the picture, ask the pair to evaluate how well the first person described the shape, how well the second person interpreted the instructions they were given and whether there were any problems in the process of communicating with one another.

Survival

In this exercise, the group must learn to communicate and agree in order to survive. The group should be told their airplane has just crashed in the ocean. A desert island is located nearby and there is room on the lifeboat for each person along with twelve items they will need in order to survive on the island. The team should be instructed to select the items they will take. How will they decide? How will they rate each item?

Eliminating Labeling

This exercise works well with a medium to large size group. Write a variety of personality types or labels on name tags using this list:

- Auto mechanic.
- Olympic medalist.
- Professor.
- Fast-food restaurant worker.
- Postal worker.
- Movie star.

Next, tape or pin a tag on each person's back but make sure they do not see what it is. Ask each person to determine which personality type is on their back by asking other people questions, such as "Am I man?" or "Am I woman?" or "Am I a celebrity?"

Team members should only be allowed to answer yes or no to questions.

The Human Spring

Ask team members to stand facing one another in pairs. Elbows should be bent and palms should be facing each other. Instruct them to touch their palms together and then begin to gradually start leaning toward one another. Eventually they should be holding up one another. Next, instruct everyone to move their feet further and further back so they must solely depend upon their partners to remain standing.

The Mine Field

This activity works well in an outdoor area or large room. Set up a mine field using cones, boxes, balls, cones, etc. Leave enough space between objects so that someone can walk through. Next, divide the group into pairs, paying careful attention to who is paired with whom. This is a good chance to work on relationships. One person in each pair will be blindfolded and become the mine walker.

This person will not be allowed to talk. Their partner must stay outside the mine field and provide verbal directions by helping the mine walker to avoid the obstacles and reach the other side of the mine field. Before beginning, make sure each pair of partners is given a few minutes to plan how they will communicate with one another. Consequences should be provided for people who do hit an obstacle, such as start over from the beginning.

Massage Circle

Begin by having the team form a circle so that everyone is facing the center and is lined up shoulder to shoulder. Next, ask everyone to turn to their right and take a step toward the center of the circle. This will make the circle tighter. Now, everyone should reach forward and give the person a shoulder massage. After a few minutes, everyone will turn to the opposite direction and do the same.

The Human Knot

A group of at least four people will be needed for this exercise. The larger the group, the more difficult this exercise will be. Team members should form a circle so that everyone is facing one another. Ask everyone to reach across and grab two hands of different people. This will form the knot. The objective is to untangle the knot without releasing hands. Members may climb or step over the hands as they try to untangle themselves. When finished, no one's hand should be connected through the middle. A new circle will be formed instead.

Stranded on an Island

The group should be broken into teams of three to four people. Teams should be instructed they are stranded on a dessert island. Ask the teams what items they would have brought with them if they could have brought only seven items. After about ten minutes, have them share with the other group members what they would have brought and explain why.

Roses and Thorns

Have each member of the team state two things they like about their team and one thing they do not like about the team while also offering a solution. Personal attacks should not be allowed.

Hula Hoop

Have the team form a circle and hold hands. Place a hula hoop inside a pair of joined hands and then ask the group to pass the hula hoop around the circle without releasing their hands. This activity can be made more challenging by passing around two or three hula hoops in the circle and having them going in different directions. The hula hoops should be different sizes so they can be easily passed through one another.

The Bridge

Break the team into two groups. Have the groups stand on opposite sides of a bridge. The bridge can be a long piece of wood, paper, etc. The goal is for each group to reach the opposite side without going back to their own side. If anyone falls off the bridge the groups must start over. Each group must work together to strategize to accomplish the goal.

Pat on the Back

Have the team form a line so they are all facing the same direction. Ask the person at the front of the line to turn around and walk towards the back of the line. On the way back, ask everyone to give that person a pat on the back. Repeat the process until everyone has received a pat on the back. You could also do hand shakes or high fives rather than a pat on the back.

Chapter 6

Ice Breakers for Team Building

Ice breakers can also be a good opportunity for team building as well as provide a fun way to help new team members get to know one another better and feel more comfortable interacting with one another. Excellent opportunities for an ice breaker including during the beginning of a meeting or conference and after people have returned from a break.

Two Truths and a Lie

Go around the room and ask each person to state two true statements about themselves and one false statement. After each person makes their statements, the other members must try and figure out which statement is the lie. The other members are allowed to ask a limited number of questions to determine which statement is false.

Toilet Paper Game

Pass a roll of toilet tissue around the room. Tell everyone to take as much paper as they like and after everyone has at least one square, have them go around the room and share one fact about themselves for each square they have taken.

Interview and Introductions

Ask everyone to pair up. Each person will take three or four minutes interviewing their partner and at the end of that time, they will introduce them to the rest of the group and at the end of that time, they will introduce them to the rest of the group.

Animals

Write down the names of animals that make a particular noise. Hand out the different slips of paper to everyone and tell them they must find the people that have the same animal. They are not allowed to talk. Most people will make gestures or animal noises, which can be a fun way to get people acquainted with one another.

The Last Line

Split everyone into groups. Give them a silly sentence written on a piece of paper. Tell them they must make up a story and act out that story with the ending of the story containing the sentence they have been given.

Line Up

Split everyone into groups of at least five and tell them to get in line in order of their birthdays or alphabetically by their first name. They must do this without talking. The first group that is able to finish wins.

Name Game

Form a circle. The first person to go will state a word they believe describes themselves and that begins with the first letter of their name and is followed by their first name. Such as Happy Hilary or Tall Tom. The following people need to state all of the previous people's name and then give their own. If anyone makes a mistake, the previous person that went must repeat their turn and the game will continue. The last person who goes will state everyone's name and then add their own name.

Orange Pass

The group will be divided into two teams and each team will line up. An orange will be placed beneath the chin of the first person in line of each time. They must hold the orange between their chest and their chin. When the game begins, the orange must be passed all the way down the line without anyone using their hands or dropping the orange. If someone does drop the orange or uses their hand, they must begin from the beginning of the line. The first team that is able to reach the end of the line will win.

Styrofoam Tower

Divide the participants into groups of between two and four people. Give each group twenty Styrofoam cups. The group that is able to construct the highest tower within five minutes will win.

Scavenger Hunt

A scavenger hunt can be a great way to build a team. You will need a list of scavenger items as well as bags. In a traditional scavenger hunt each team will receive a list of items they must collect. The team to collect all of the items in the shortest amount of time will win the challenge. Begin by compiling a list of ten to fifteen items to be collected. You might consider staggering the start times or mixing up the order of the items on the list so that teams do not arrive at one location at the same time. The list of items for the scavenger list can be almost anything but should include items that can be found relatively easily in the location of the hunt. Some ideas might include:

- A local bus schedule
- Any document issued by the government
- A state map
- A copy of the front page of the local newspaper
- A library card
- A shopping bag from a local mall
- Anything with the colors of the local high school

Questions

Simple questions can also be a good way to get people talking to one another and sharing. Consider the following ideas:

- What makes you different from other people?
- What would your dream vacation be?
- What would you do with a million dollars?
- If you could have dinner with anyone who would it be and why?
- What are you most proud of?
- What is your most valued possession and why?
- If you were an animal, what would you be and why?
- What is one goal you would like to accomplish during your lifetime?
- Who is your hero and why?
- What is your favorite thing to do during the summer/fall/winter?
- If a movie was made of your life, what would it be about and which actor would play you?
- If you were an ice cream flavor, what would it be?

- If you could visit anywhere in the world, where would you choose and why?
- What's the weirdest thing you've ever eaten?
- If you had to describe yourself using three words, what would they be?
- What is the best book you've ever read and why?
- What is the name is the best movie you've ever seen and why?
- If you could change one thing about yourself what would it be? Why?
- What do you like to do most with a free hour?
- Choose a word that best describes your life.
- What is the most beautiful thing you have ever seen?

Chapter 7

Team Building Ideas and Activities

Below are some simple ideas that can be used to assist in team building.

Team Progress Boards

You can chart the progress of a team on a large board. Continually being able to see the board can provide an excellent incentive for the team to work harder.

Team Incentives/Bonuses

Whenever a team reaches a certain milestone or completes a project, award the entire team. Incentives and awards might include a nice dinner, free movie tickets, etc.

Team News

Try posting important news on a bulletin board. You could also send it out through an email newsletter so that everyone will remain informed of the latest news on the team and no one will feel left out.

Team Name

Try choosing a team name that will help in building team unity and pride.

T-shirts

Reinforce team pride and unity with team t-shirts.

Group Activities

Plan group activities where everyone will have an opportunity to participate such as paint ball or bowling.

Group Lunch

Organize a team lunch outside of work where everyone will be able to sit together and interact outside of the workplace.

Retreats

Team retreats can also be a great way to build your team, particularly if you go to a retreat with a team building curriculum that is provided.

Social Outings

Social outings can also provide a stress free environment and allow team members to socialize regarding topics that are not work related while building their relationships on a personal level.

Consider options such as:

- Barbecue,
- Family picnic at the park
- Lunchtime drink
- Bowling
- Playing paint ball
- Quiz night

Sports

Sports are an excellent way to form bonds within a team. The key is to include everyone and not just the best players.

Chapter 8

Mistakes to Avoid

There are a few things that should be avoided in team building in order to have the most effectiveness and build the strongest team possible. First, keep in mind that team building should occur on a continual basis in order to be effective. Team building exercises should be incorporated on a weekly or at least a monthly routine. This will assist everyone in addressing different issues and will also offer the opportunity to everyone to have some fun and learn to trust one another.

In addition, you should make sure that team building exercises are not competitive in nature. Competition will only make the members of your team work against one another and that will impede the building of unity.

You should also make sure that there are always issues or challenges which are identified and need to be worked upon. This will help to ensure that the team gains some benefits from the team building exercises. Remember, team building activities should always have a point and should not be performed simply for the sake of doing them.

Never expect a new team to be ready to act like one from the very first day. Every team has its own entity and will need time for development. Do not exercise tight management control. This will only hinder creativity. Do not allow the team to feel too exclusive as this can cause other parts of the organization to feel left out. Do not let individuals take credit for the achievements of the team.

TEAM EFFECTIVENESS CRITIQUE

Indicate below your assessment of your team and how it functions by circling a number that you feel best describes your team.

1. GOALS AND OBJECTIVES
Team members understand and agree on goals and objectives
1 2 3 4 5

2. UTILIZATION OF RESOURCES
All team member resources are recognized and/or utilized
1 2 3 4 5

3. TRUST AND CONFLICT
There is a high degree of trust among team members and conflict is handled in an effective manner
1 2 3 4 5

4. LEADERSHIP
There is full participation by all team members and leadership is shared by all team members.
1 2 3 4 5

5. CONTROL AND PROCEDURES
There are effective procedures in place to guide the functions of the team. Team members support these procedures.
1 2 3 4 5

6. INTERPERSONAL COMMUNICATIONS
Communications between team members are open and fully participatory.
1 2 3 4 5

7. PROBLEM SOLVING/DECISION MAKING
The team has well-established approaches to problem solving and decision making.
1 2 3 4 5

8. EXPERIMENTATION/CREATIVITY
The team experiments with new and different methods and is creative in its approach.
1 2 3 4 5

9. EVALUATION
The group often evaluates processes and functions.
1 2 3 4 5

10. ROLES AND RESPONSIBILITIES
The team members have a good sense of their roles and responsibilities.
1 2 3 4 5

TEAM BUILDING NEEDS ASSESSMENT

The following needs assessment will help your team to reduce the gap between the current status and the way things should be within your team. Whether it is your goal to produce better results, better standards, better performance or better procedures, this needs assessment will help in building a more effective team building process.

Identifying Team Building Needs

Ask team members to write down a pressing need, issue or problem. Team members may focus on existing needs or something they would like to see addressed over the short-term. Allow all team members to review each of the needs and then combine those needs, narrow them and then rank them in order of priority. The team should choose the need that is most pertinent.

Clarifying Team Needs

Ask the team members to address these questions:

- Why is it necessary to address this need?
- What will happen if this need is not addressed?
- How widespread is this need?
- How long has this need been an issue?

- How has this need impacted the team or organization?
- Is this a need the team can actually improve or correct?

Root Causes

For more productive actions to be made, it is important to understand the causes at the root of the current problem. Have the team discuss these questions:
- How did this problem arise?
- What perpetuates this problem?
- To what extent is this problem a performance issue?
- Is this problem structural or process related?
- Is this problem a financial issue?
- this problem a training/knowledge issue?
- Is this problem a personnel issue?

Identifying Possible Solutions and/or Interventions

Ask the team to identify possible solutions to address the problem. Complete the following:

- Specifically define the solution
- Explain how the solution addresses the root cause of the problem
- Identify the tools and resources necessary for this solution

- Identify persons or groups that must be involved
- Clarify how the solution fits in with the goals of the team and organization
- Identify signs of success. How will the solution be gauged as working?

Prioritization

Ask the team to discuss all possible solutions. Next, ask the team to prioritize those solutions and determine which will be implemented. Assign one person to each solution who will be responsible for establishing time lines, identifying milestones and determining how the effectiveness of the solution will be assessed.

TEAM FOCUS ASSESSMENT

The following tool can be used for assessing the current status of your team to assist in determining where your team needs to be focused.

The following scale should be used: 1= weak; 2= needs strengthening; 3= average; 4= good; 5= very strong

Rating	Question
1 2 3 4 5	Does your team have a clear and defined purpose for existing?
1 2 3 4 5	Are your knowledge and skills a good match for your team?
1 2 3 4 5	Do you feel as though you can rely on team members?
1 2 3 4 5	Do team members interact in a trusting and open manner?
1 2 3 4 5	Does your team have goals that are specific and clear?
1 2 3 4 5	Does your team have values that are clear and established?
1 2 3 4 5	Are decision protocols in place for your team?
1 2 3 4 5	Does your team solve problems in an efficient manner?
1 2 3 4 5	Are action items executed in an efficient manner?
1 2 3 4 5	Does the team consistently meet and exceed expectations?
1 2 3 4 5	Is the team able to change efficiently?
1 2 3 4 5	Does the team take time to celebrate and renew core values?

WORK SATISFACTION INVENTORY

How effective and productive are individual contributors in your team? How do you rate your own contributions? The assessment below will help you to gauge your work satisfaction.

Meaning

In the ideal job the contributor's sense of meaning is enhanced. Work has value and heightens the contributor's sense of self-worth and achievement.

1	2	3	4	5
Low				High

Satisfaction

Contributors seek the happiness that is associated with a job well done. Contributors work towards finding a solution or resolution to problems. Achievement of goals provides a sense of success.

1	2	3	4	5
Low				High

Impact

Contributors like to make a difference and feel as though they have made the organization more successful. Contributors feel as though their work contributes to their professional development.

1	2	3	4	5
Low				**High**

Recognition

Contributors like to be recognized for their strengths and skills.

1	2	3	4	5
Low				**High**

Relationships

Contributors are interested in forming connections with others by laughing, celebrating, solving problems and even struggling with others.

1	2	3	4	5
Low				**High**

Assessment

Add up the totals for each question and then divide by five. The average should provide a general idea regarding each team member's sense of their own contribution to the organization.

Scoring Guidelines

If your average score is between 1 and 2.5; your sense of contribution to your organization is low. If your average score is between 2.6 and 3.5, your feelings regarding your contribution to your organization are mixed. You may find it helpful to look for ways you can improve the value of your responsibilities. If your average score is between 3.6 and 5, you have a productive sense of what you contribute to your organization.

Other books by Psylon Press:

100% Blonde Jokes
R. Cristi
ISBN 978-0-9866004-1-8

Choosing a Dog Breed Guide
Eric Nolah
ISBN 978-0-9866004-5-6

Best Pictures Of Paris
Christian Radulescu
ISBN 978-0-9866004-8-7

Best Gift Ideas For Women
Taylor Timms
ISBN 978-0-9866004-4-9

Top Bikini Pictures
Taylor Timms
ISBN 978-0-9866426-3-0

Cross Tattoos
Johnny Karp
ISBN 978-0-9866426-4-7

Beautiful Breasts Pictures
Taylor Timms
ISBN 978-1-926917-01-6

For more books please visit:
www.psylonpress.com

www.ingramcontent.com/pod-product-compliance
Lightning Source LLC
LaVergne TN
LVHW051850080426
835512LV00018B/3173